Finding Your Pattern
For Peace:

Choosing a Healthy Normal

SARAH FREEMAN, M.A., LPCC

SARAH FREEMAN

ISBN: 1517372763
ISBN-13: 978-1517372767

DEDICATION

This book is dedicated to those who eagerly welcome the next chapter in their lives; greeting each day with strength and courage.

I am forever grateful to my family, friends, and colleagues for the encouragement to publish my ideas about self-care. It is with great appreciation that I recognize the Bridge to Recovery for supporting my personal and professional growth. A special thanks to Megan Gammon Algie B.A., Heather Webb CSW, Anna Waycoff, Dr. Suzy Coykendall, Ph.D., and Tim Freeman. Megan, your attention to detail and enthusiasm about this project was the final push towards publication. You graciously provided support when I was feeling overwhelmed and struggling to move forward. Heather, thank you for being so generous with the time and energy you spent revising and making sense out of my ideas. Your contribution provided clarity and motivation. Anna, I am so grateful for your willingness to illustrate the concepts in a fun and creative way and for being such a longstanding part of my life. We have such an extraordinary friendship! Suzy, thank you for believing in me and being my mentor at a time when I needed direction. You will never know how much of an impact you make in the lives of your students. Finally, Tim Freeman, thank you for riding this roller coaster with me and endlessly supporting my projects.

CONTENTS

	Introduction	2
1	What is Normal	4
2	Peaceful Normal vs Chaotic Normal	11
3	Giver and Taker Relationships	18
4	For Parents	31
5	Toxic Box	35
6	Is It Science?	40
7	Isolation	51
8	Choose Your Healthy Normal	56
9	Finding Your Pattern	62
10	U-turns and Warming Flags	70
11	Two Week Challenge	77
12	Two Week Challenge Example	81
13	Practicing My Pattern	85
14	Continued Practice	94
	Appendix	98
	From the Author	101

INTRODUCTION

This book was created for you; not the you that resembles the ever-changing chameleon constantly adapting to the environment, but the true and authentic YOU. It was designed to be a guide that reunites you with the light seated at the center of your being. Your light is powerful, beautiful, and real. Your light is your sanctuary within and needs to be trusted as your guide to a more fulfilling and abundant life.

Finding Your Pattern for Peace will help you begin to discover and enforce a practice of self-love. Your practice commences with self-awareness and the confidence that your authentic self is the direct route to living a peaceful and grounded existence. The process described in this book necessitates individuation and customization. It is a workbook with space for coloring and doodling. The combination of these components promotes creativity, thoughtfulness, and personalization. The addition of color ensures that your story embraces intellectual, emotional, and visual inspiration. Please customize your experience by adding color, drawings, inspirations, thoughts, profanities, etc. The illustrations in this workbook were graciously created and donated by Anna Waychoff. Her contribution promotes a space in which vulnerability and personal expression is safe, encouraged, and honored.

You will find *thought spots* throughout the following chapters encouraging expression of your thoughts and opinions as they evolve throughout your journey. These spaces may also be helpful in displacing nervous energy as you find yourself relating to various concepts throughout the text. Do not feel confined to stay within in the lines of the boxes. There are *no* rules when expressing your truth and *all* truths are welcomed. Liberate yourself from the expectations and rules that restrict you from living authentically. Enjoy this journey. Honor all you have endured that led you to this point. Now is your time to sort through the pieces of your life and discard anything that does not serve or support your desired future narrative. Sorting through your pieces will illuminate your definition of *normal* and will serve as a compass to finding *your* personal pattern for peace.

You already possess everything

necessary to become great.

~ Native American Proverb

1. WHAT IS NORMAL

Healthy people make self-care a priority to promote a happy life and fulfilling relationships. It is your responsibility to maintain self-care, as this becomes your foundation for normal. This foundation promotes freedom to enjoy your life, find activities that make you happy, and spend time with people who support and care for you. This workbook is about learning to feed yourself, love yourself and create a healthy space, so you can experience the world and fulfill your greater purpose.

You create a guideline allowing you to base your normal on *your* standards, rather than the standards of others. If you feel bad, check in with yourself. There's a good chance you are foregoing your self-care. This concept is not meant to be a perfect model or something that is practiced the same way each day. Just do your best and know that you have something to fall back on when life gets messy. Be aware that your normal changes from time to time and make adjustments as needed. Life forces transition and it is easier to adapt when there is a sense of stability.

Finding Your Pattern for Peace will give you comfort in knowing that your stability comes from within. You will feel liberated when you no longer *need* others to feel complete, allowing you to experience genuine love and intimacy with the people in your life. You will feel relief when your space becomes a sanctuary, a place that is honored and safe. You will find *you* and it will be beautiful!

This workbook intends to help you discover what truly amplifies your higher purpose. It is not a difficult task. It is solidified through awareness, consistency, and discipline. The outcome is worth the effort. You are worth the effort.

Each individual has a personal **normal,** defined herein as any habit, routine, reaction, or world view that consistently occurs in our daily living and the life patterns developed from these behaviors. However, normal does not necessarily equate to healthy. Many patterns are unhealthy due to high levels of dysfunction and chaos. The goal of *Finding Your Pattern for Peace* is to assist you in discovering your healthy version of normal. In this book **healthy** is defined as stable life patterns that cultivate a peaceful and balanced life. **Unhealthy** is defined as unstable life patterns that foster a chaotic and unfulfilling life.

A healthy normal is primarily *self-focused* and an unhealthy normal is primarily *others-focused. Finding Your Pattern for Peace* may sound like shameless, self-promotion but be assured that it is not. The concept of being self-focused emphasizes our individual responsibility to maintain a foundation of self-care in order to promote the most fulfilling version of our life. As self-focused individuals, we are able to recognize and make our unique needs a priority while respecting the needs and values of others.

Healthy relationships are a cornerstone to satisfied living. Socializing, belonging, and caring for others are basic human needs. These needs, also fulfill moral and social responsibilities. When one is able to maintain self-care, they are able to find a level of richness in their lives and relationships that they never thought possible.

Being others-focused creates dependency on others for validation, self-worth, confidence, and approval. This dependency limits self-regulation and extinguishes personal empowerment. Being others-focused will only result in disillusionment, as our worth is based on performance rather than authenticity.

In summary, being self-focused is a term used to describe the role of self-care as an essential factor in the promotion of a healthy and authentic lifestyle. In contrast, being others-focused bases fulfillment and life satisfaction on the ever-changing reactions and expectations (real or

perceived) of others.

The first step to finding your healthy normal is understanding what being healthy means to you. Jot down your thoughts in the space below.

_____

_____

_____

_____

_____

_____

_____

_____

_____

_____

_____

_____

_____

_____

Self-preservation is the first law of nature.

~English Proverb

Throughout this text, healthy life patterns refer to practices that support and serve your higher purpose. We all have different values, wants, and needs. These differences necessitate finding a personal path to create and maintain genuine and healthy life pattern for yourself.

Think back to when you were a child. It is likely that you remember an exciting and hopeful world ready to be explored. Write about a specific memory that reminds you of this happier world. Describe in the space below what it was like for you and how it felt. If you cannot recall a positive memory, think of a current event or activity that makes you feel alive, such as; laughing with friends, spending time with loved ones, prayer, playing with pets, singing, exercising, etc.

_____

_____

_____

_____

_____

_____

_____

_____

_____

Imagine what your life would be like if directed from this authentic space…

How would you feel?

What would you do differently?

What would it look like to others?

How would you respond to others?

For some, the excitement for life fizzled due to social training and expectations from peers, culture, religious influence, media, and families. This social conditioning can result in a world-view that happiness and life satisfaction are dependent on the response we get from others.

This conditioning is similar to housebreaking a dog, and will be referred to as *life-breaking*. We are life-broken when we lose our natural tendency to live and love freely without fear or reservation. By reclaiming our higher purpose, we return to viewing the world from a perspective of hope and optimism.

What prevents you from living your life from this perspective consistently? What is blocking your path?

_____

_____

_____

_____

_____

Can you recall an event that precipitated being life-broken?

_____

_____

_____

_____

_____

_____

_____

What messages were you given that resulted in a belief system that you are not "ok"? (Example: People will leave me if I tell them "no.")

1. _____

_____

2. _____

_____

3. _____

_____

4. _____

_____

5. _____

_____

_____

_____

Write an opposing message to each of the statements listed above. (Example: I know 3 people who respect me when I say "no.")

1. _____

_____

2. _____

_____

3. _____

_____

4. _____

_____

5. _____

_____

_____

2. PEACEFUL NORMAL VS. CHAOTIC NORMAL

We will begin by looking at the difference between our peaceful and chaotic experiences. As you look at the columns on the following pages, mark the characteristics that describe your common tendencies. Once this is completed, add your total marks and write the number at the bottom of the column.

Peaceful Normal Characteristics	Chaotic Normal Characteristics
o I am confident and secure about my identity.	o I am insecure and lack confidence about my identity.
o I am comfortable and proactive about making decisions.	o I seek validation and often look to others when making decisions.
o I have stable, positive, and healthy relationships.	o My relationships are unstable.
o I enjoy a variety of activities.	o I struggle to identify specific activities that I sincerely enjoy.
o I am comfortable being alone.	o I am uncomfortable when I am alone.
o I am able to balance work, social life, and self-care.	o I struggle with finding balance between work, social life, and self-care.
o I feel that I live a purposeful life.	o I feel that my life lacks purpose.
o I experience a full range of emotions.	o My emotions are either numb or extreme (i.e. great or awful).
o I feel that others see and respect me.	o I feel like I have to beg others to see or respect me.
o I do not require validation from others.	

o I am comfortable when others express their feelings. o I am optimistic about my future. o I trust the intentions of others. o I say "no" and set limits when needed. o I hold others accountable when they cross my boundaries. o I have self respect. o I engage in playful and fun activities. o I feel fulfilled. o I feel authentic and genuine in my daily interaction with others and myself.	o I'm always trying to prove myself. o Intimacy scares me. o I am pessimistic about my future. o I am worried that others have a hidden agenda. o I make excuses about negative behaviors displayed by others and struggle to set limits. o Feeling sorry for people gets me in trouble. o I feel guilty when I do things for myself. o I expect things to go wrong, especially when things are going well. o I feel desperate. o Many times I feel like my life is a performance which results in a sense of "walking on eggshells" when I am around others.
Total: _____	Total: _____

Next, give examples of places where you experience peaceful and chaotic characteristics.

Places where I experience peace:	Places where I experience chaos:
o Home	o Home
o School	o School
o Work	o Work
o Church	o Church
o _____	o _____
o _____	o _____
o _____	o _____
o _____	o _____
o _____	o _____

Finally, list the individuals who illicit both peaceful and chaotic feelings within you.

When I am around the following individuals I tend to feel peaceful.	When I am around the following individuals I tend to feel chaotic.
o _____	o _____
o _____	o _____
o _____	o _____
o _____	o _____
o _____	o _____
o _____	o _____
o _____	o _____

Your Patterns

If you scored higher on the right column, your pattern is likely to be unhealthy, leaving you feeling that your life is unfulfilling and chaotic. This pattern may also limit your ability to live a life that feels meaningful. If you scored higher on the left column, you are inclined to have a healthier, more peaceful, pattern as well as a self-awareness that you are actively working to maintain.

You are likely to identify with qualities from both columns. In considering the differences between the two columns, let's look at the relationships between people and places that trigger your feelings of worth. Recognizing the people with whom you feel peaceful and the places where you feel grounded provides a model for future relationships and behaviors.

What is unique about the places where you feel peaceful vs. chaotic? How are you different in those places?

_____

_____

_____

_____

_____

What is unique about the people with whom you feel peaceful vs. chaotic? How are you different with those people?

_____

_____

_____

_____

_____

In summary, relationships locked in a chaotic pattern are primarily others-focused. This dynamic is commonly referred to as codependency, or as defined by Melody Beattie, "a dysfunctional relationship in which a person is more concerned about the needs of others than his or her own needs. It is often characterized by excessive care-taking or enabling, and an unhealthy need for recognition or approval."[1]

Chaotic relationship patterns or codependent relationships can be described as a 90/10 split. One person, referred to as the **giver**, tends to provide 90% of the effort in a relationship, whereas the other person, referred to as the **taker**, provides 10% of the effort. In a single relationship, it is not uncommon for these roles to vacillate, resulting in an inequitable power struggle rather than true intimacy and connection.

Identify and describe a relationship that you consider unbalanced in emotional contribution.

_____

_____

_____

_____

_____

_____

_____

_____

_____

_____

_____

• [1] Beattie, M. (1987). Codependent No More: How to Stop Controlling Others and Start Caring for Yourself. Center City, MN: Hazelden Publishing.

THOUGHT SPOT

Do not treat your loved one like a swinging door:

do not push it back and forth.

~ Malagasy Proverb

Describe a time when you have identified as a giver in a relationship, meaning you put forth 90% of the effort. What was the motivation for the relationship?

_____

_____

_____

_____

_____

_____

_____

Describe a time when you have identified as a taker in a relationship, meaning you put forth 10% of the effort. What was the motivation for the relationship?

_____

_____

_____

_____

_____

_____

_____

Which role is your status-quo, meaning which role are you more likely to play?

_____

_____

_____

_____

_____

_____

3. GIVER AND TAKER RELATIONSHIPS

Takers – Those who receive more energy than give in a relationship.

Toxic Takers

The toxic taker is an individual that failed to learn how to fully care for themselves or others. They have managed to give very little in relationships in order to be treated well. It is common for these individuals to assume that others will naturally make adjustments to meet their needs. Often times, these individuals desire mutual relations but struggle to comprehend the process of reciprocity, which is a critical component in healthy relationships.

Research shows that individuals raised by neglectful or uninvolved parents struggle with social competence and development including reciprocity, social norms, self-regulation, boundaries, and empathy.[2] These individuals often expect others to understand them and make adjustments to suit their needs and moods. These individuals typically become toxic takers exhibiting low levels of a sense of entitlement and little regard for others.

The toxic taker is a challenge because an individual who failed to learn basic social skills often struggles to settle into a healthy relationship with themselves and with others. It is not uncommon for these individuals to jump from one relationship to the next in order to have their needs met. Toxic takers often confuse the concept of a relationship with emotional slavery.

---

[2] Darling, Nancy. (1999). Parenting style and its correlates. ERIC Digest. Champaign, IL: ERIC Clearinghouse on Elementary and Early Childhood Education. (ERIC Document No. ED427896). Also available: http://ericeece.org/pubs/digests/1999/ darlin99.html.

Immobilized Takers

The immobilized taker often feels overwhelmed and insecure when making decisions, being alone, or following through with tasks of all sizes. When friends and partners express interest in other relationships, a sense of jealousy, fear, or frustration emerges due to a perceived lack of support and an inability to meet their own needs. This pattern emerges when an individual is overly protected, enabled, and given unlimited support. This abundance of support may be the result of childhood mental or physical limitations and a caregiver's desire to provide a supportive environment. The intention of the support is positive but not allowing a child to experience growing pains can result in immobilization. This is a painful pattern that will continue if it is not addressed. When a giver is no longer able to provide support the immobilized taker feels lost, and may experience a sense of aimlessness leading to emotions ranging from frustration to desperation.

After reading about the giver/taker pattern, a colleague suggested that she was a taker but not intentionally as she truly desires to contribute more to her relationships. She recognized that others rescue her any time they observe her struggling with common life challenges. The same individual expressed feelings of insecurity and uncertainty related to making decisions due to her loved ones always having cushioned her with the intention of setting her up for success.

He who conquers others is strong.

He who conquers himself is mighty.

~ Zen Proverb

THOUGHT SPOT

I'll gladly pay you Tuesday

for a hamburger today.

~ Cartoon Catchphrase, Advertising, TV

Givers – Those who give more energy than they receive in a relationship.

Toxic Givers

At some level, the toxic giver may understand the taker's limitations for self-care. They may understand that dependency can be established through excessive giving. This type of giver may also feel that the dependency they promote creates a sense of purpose rationalizing a role of martyrdom. Unfortunately, this dynamic perpetuates an ongoing cycle of codependency resulting in a painful and confusing experience where both participants feel as though they are in a stalemate.

Caretaking Givers

The caretaking giver sincerely wants the best for the taker and experiences a sense of discomfort when they witness their loved one struggling to navigate various life obstacles. This type of giving is based in love and a desire to be supportive, but also creates fear and discomfort for the individual who needs to learn self-care. This dynamic is maladaptive, negating the taker's effort at autonomy, as described with the immobilized taker. There is a difference in care-taking and care-giving. Specifically, care-taking, sabotages one's efforts to care for themselves whereas care-giving provides support; without enabling and creating codependency.[3]

As one individual expressed, "It is hard for me to feel motivated to take care of myself when others around me are so competent and do it for me. I do not cook, clean, pay bills, or read mail. My mom even helps me throw birthday parties and baby showers. Once a year she helps me reorganize my things. I have never bought a car, etc."

---

[3] Kupeferman, Elizabeth. Codependency: Caretaking vs. Caregiving. Retrieved from http://www.expressivecounseling.com/codependency-caretaking/

If a loved one is accustomed to having everything done for them, they will struggle to achieve independence. Allowing them to struggle, while providing support through encouragement and understanding one can promote their loved one's transition to independence. However, enabling them only prolongs the process they must undergo to achieve positive growth. If you choose to address your caretaking behaviors, try to avoid attaching personal responsibility to your loved one's behaviors and/or successes. It is common to experience a sense of loss when the person you have so intensely supported is now caring for themselves. Your support is still needed, just in a different way. With a few adjustments and a refocus on your self-care, the relationship has the potential to grow beyond its previous limitations.

Broken Givers

The broken giver is deeply hurt and often maintains a belief system that is indicative of an identity based on pleasing others. The broken giver puts countless hours, work, and energy into serving others. This behavior often stems from extreme insecurity and feelings of desperation, due to personal value being linked to receiving validation from others. Unfortunately, the effort is rarely acknowledged or rewarded, as hoped for, resulting in feelings of low self-worth, disappointment, fear, and inferiority.

In spite of the overt and covert messages you received throughout your lifetime, it is critical for your emotional, mental, spiritual, and physical well-being to seize your birthright of living an authentic life.

A scholar's ink lasts longer than

a martyr's blood.

~ Irish Proverb

Reflect on your experience as a giver or taker. It is common to play both roles depending on life situations but more often than not you will be able to identify more with one over the other.

_____

_____

_____

_____

_____

=======================================

What situations trigger giver behaviors vs. taker behaviors?

_____

_____

_____

_____

_____

=======================================

What situations trigger taker behaviors vs. giver behaviors?

_____

_____

_____

_____

_____

_____

=======================================

How does being a giver or taker serve you? What are the benefits?

_____

_____

_____

_____

_____

_____

_____

═══

How does being a giver or taker prove to be a disservice to your overall wellbeing?

_____

_____

_____

_____

_____

_____

_____

_____

_____

_____

═══

THOUGHT SPOT

What you think you are, you are,

until you think otherwise.

~ American Proverb

Giving Cupcakes & Taking Cupcakes

Allow your inner child to imagine the taker/giver or 90/10 relationship as cupcakes. In this type of relationship there are two regular sized cupcakes but one has no frosting (*giving cupcake*) while the other has double the frosting (*taking cupcake*). Essentially, the giving cupcake provided the taking cupcake with extra frosting by giving all that it had to the other cupcake. The giver waits for the frosting to be returned by the taker, but the taker is clueless about this exchange. In fact, the taker is so accustomed to being overloaded with frosting that it fails to comprehend the effort or sacrifice of the giver. The taker's lack of regard for the time and energy used to provide so much frosting leaves the giver feeling disappointed and rejected.

The giver puts forth significant effort but nevertheless overwhelms the taker, causing them to struggle to hold so much frosting at one time. This results in the giver feeling unappreciated and confused. The lack of response from the *taker* results in the *giver* feeling like the taker was not satisfied and is in need of more *frosting*.

This perpetual dynamic is exhausting; the taker doesn't need to put forth much effort to be emotionally fed or cared for, causing them to not understand what it is like to be emotionally hungry. The taker finds it difficult to fully appreciate the work involved in feeding and caring for another person. The giver stays exhausted seeking validation and appreciation from the taker, which unlikely come.

If one gives all their *frosting* away and leaves none for themselves, they will remain hungry. The expectation of reciprocity fuels feelings of obligation. The thinking process may be similar to, "I gave all this frosting to you. Aren't you going to do the same for me?" The disparity in contribution can lead to feelings of doubt, anger, sadness, and confusion. The dynamic does not benefit the giver or the taker because the taker's *perceived* hunger is only a projection of the emptiness felt by the giver. The giver does not recognize the taker's lack of hunger. The giver's own need to be fed keeps them hopeful that one day their effort will be reciprocated.

Only when the giver practices self-care does the taker become anxious about losing their supplier. The taker then offers the giver the emotional support they have craved. This effort often leaves the giver feeling momentarily valued but it promotes a return to the status quo. Although there are vast differences between givers and takers, their commonality of *fear* perpetuates these roles and paralyzes healthy growth. Furthermore, this fear leads to high instances of role-reversal, in which each person plays the role of the giver and the taker. The switching of roles is essentially a change of power in the dynamic of the relationship. The taker is in the position of power and the giver is left feeling inferior.

Love your neighbor, but don't

tear down your fence.

~ German Proverb

THOUGHT SPOT

Wonder is the beginning of wisdom.

~ Ancient proverb

4. FOR PARENTS

In a 90/10 relationship between a parent and child, where the parent gives 90%, the child struggles to comprehend concepts including empathy, respect, perseverance, independence, and reciprocity in relationships. The 90/10 dynamic either teaches the child that they are entitled to anything they desire or by role-modelling the parent they learn that it is necessary to always put others first in order to feel worthy. Parents – we teach children how to be adults! Teach them to say *no* by saying *"no."*

If the parent is giving 10% and expecting 90% from their child, it is likely that the child will be dependent on others for a sense of value. Parenting is difficult and the strategies used complete this bittersweet task are often automatic and unconscious. However, if you are a parent, you may want to consider how it will feel when your child becomes an adult and seeks relationships that reenact the "normalcy" learned in childhood. Consider the following questions:

- Are you comfortable with someone treating your child the way you treat him or her?

- Do you want your child treating others like you treat him or her?

- What role expectations are you creating by your action or lack of action?

Role-reversal has serious implications on a child's development because it ingrains a belief system that self-care is a response to a crisis, and caring for others is critical for survival. It is the responsibility of the parents to support for a child not the opposite.

Many parents mourn as they watch their children jump from one painful relationship to another. Some parents identify ways in which they unintentionally role-modeled the exact behaviors they are witnessing in their children. Obviously, the perfect parent does not exist but awareness of your intentions will increase the success of this process. It is normal to make mistakes and it is normal to recover from them through communication and action. Again, we teach our children how to be adults and it is absurd to think that children will learn how take responsibility for their actions if it is not demonstrated. It is not a sign of weakness to apologize or make amends when you make a mistake. An apology perpetuates mutual respect and an example of the expectations of both the child and the adult.

A healthy parent/child relationship is one that promotes a sense of stability, respect for self and others, boundaries, and celebration of autonomy. Research suggests that the most effective parenting style is authoritative.[4] This parenting style is more democratic in nature as the child has rules and expectations but also feels supported and is given freedom to make decisions and mistakes. This promotes connections between behaviors and consequences hence teaching personal responsibility and creating realistic expectations in all areas of life.

Describe the relationship between you and your parents?

_____

_____

_____

_____

_____

_____

---

[4] Steinberg, L., Elmen, J., & Mounts, N. (1989). Authoritative Parenting, Psychosocial Maturity, and Academic Success among Adolescents. *Child Development*, *60*(6), 1424-1436. doi:1. Retrieved from http://www.jstor.org/stable/1130932 doi:1

How did the dynamic between you and your parents affect your ability to...

Make decisions:

Receive love:

Show love:

Experience confidence:

Depend on others:

Set and respect boundaries:

Function socially:

Engage in self-care:

Communicate:

Solve problems:

Say "No":

Experience success:

Experience set backs:

Take care of basic needs:

Engage in play:

Make friends:

Work:

What does a 90/10 parent/child relationship look like to you?

_____

_____

_____

_____

_____

_____

What does a 50/50 parent/child relationship look like to you?

_____

_____

_____

_____

_____

What are your views on the best practice for parenting from an adult's perspective?

_____

_____

_____

_____

_____

_____

The young man shows what the old man was.

~ Swedish Proverb

5. THE TOXIC BOX

Promoting the healthiest version of yourself is reliant on having a realistic understanding of your unhealthy and healthy patterns. When exploring the characteristics of your unhealthy patterns, it is important to be open minded and honest about the situations leading you to a toxic place. This toxic place will be referred to as the **toxic box**.

The toxic box is a place where we find ourselves focusing more on the needs of others rather than our own. Residency in the toxic box can result in a myriad of negative emotions and self-defeating behaviors that prevent us from having enriching realtionships. Listed on the following page are several common indicators that one may be in a toxic relationship.

On the following page select characteristics that resemble your tendencies in relationships and life patterns.

- o I feel insecure and lack confidence with my identity.
- o I am seek approval, attention, and validation.
- o I am uncertain the status of my relationships.
- o I am uncomfortable being alone.
- o I lack balance between work, social life, and self-care.
- o I worry that my life lacks purpose.
- o I feel numb or emotional extremes.
- o I feel like I am begging to be seen or respected.
- o I am constantly proving my worth.
- o I am distrustful and feel that others have a hidden agenda.
- o I am pessimistic about the future of my relationships.
- o I excuse and justify hurtful behaviors and struggle to set limits.
- o I often feel sorry for people which leads to caretaking behaviors.
- o I feel guilty when I do nice things for myself.
- o I am nervous that something will go wrong, especially when things are going well.
- o I feel empty.
- o Many times I feel like I am a performer and constantly adapt to meet the expectations of others
- o I am at my best when I am told…

> WHO to be…   WHAT to be…   WHERE to be…
> WHEN to be…   WHY to be…   HOW to be

- o I often feel like I am "walking on eggshells."
- o I constantly worry if people are mad at me or if I did something wrong.
- o I feel out-of-control.
- o I feel like I act desperate and needy.
- o I feel emotionally starved.
- o I am exhausted.
- o I feel let down on a regular basis.
- o I spend a lot of time waiting for others to make me feel important.

It is likely that these thoughts and feelings originated from unprocessed chaos in childhood including but not limited to traumatic events, neglect, extreme chaos, limited resources, being a victim of or witness to physical, mental, and/or sexual abuse. In efforts to survive chaos, extreme coping strategies are developed. These skills are effective and adaptive in the presence of chaos, but turn destructive and counterproductive when they continue to be use as a primary solution for coping.

Metaphorically, humans create an internal emotional army during times of crisis. This army is is critical for survival and ideally when the crisis ends the army retreats to a reserve status. However, without guidance, fear and traumatic echoes from the past perpetuate the use of old tactics to cope with current situations. These tactics are ineffective and often recreate chaos that is similar to that experienced in childhood. The similarity of the current and past experiences justify the necessity of keeping old tactics sharp, essentially the original trauma is repeatedly reenacted which rationalizes a need for a skill set that can handle the never-ending emergencies.

This pattern of behavior perpetuates pain and fear resulting in an increased need for drastic forms of self-protection. If a person does not reconfigure their worldview, they will continually repeat these destructive cycles. Often times individuals are insightful that their behaviors are not productive but feel stuck on "auto-pilot" as they over react to situations in which the extreme reactions are not warranted.

For example, calling 911 because the coffee is empty is not the best strategy for obtaining a cup of coffee. However, without an understanding of other options then one does what is necessary to get a pot of coffee and expectedly suffer the consequences.

QUESTION: Why would a person continually engage in drastic behaviors when the consequences are unfavorable?

ANSWER: The process is familiar and albeit uncomfortable, it gets the job done.

The common phrase "I'm okay, if you're okay" becomes a powerful concept that promotes linking feelings of safety and security to the reactions and approval of others. This occurs when childhood lessons and life situations teach that shame, guilt, rejection, punishment, confusion, and fear are synonymous with primary relationships. These thinking patterns are the same as those of givers, who place the needs of others above their own in hopes of a positive outcome such as security, certainty, value, respect, love, and appreciation. Out of all of the potential outcomes security and certainty are the most basic and necessary for survival, the others are secondary and often overlooked. Ultimately, unhealthy normal patterns are formed in response to the prevalence of chaos and the familiar skill set used to combat the situations. The familiarity and ability to navigate tragedy drives an individual to seek chaos thus promoting a sense of certainty.

Without insight and a desire to change, these patterns will fossilize resulting in entrapment in the toxic box. It is critical that patterns are recognized and changes are made not only to promote a more peaceful life but to prevent significant self-destruction and generations of dysfunction.

The toxic box is complicated for many reasons. It is founded in both real and perceived experiences. Real expectations may develop from past experiences where punishment such as physical harm, ridicule, or neglect were a consequence of self-expression, boundary setting, or self-care. Real expectations may also involve making unreasonable demands or requests, resulting in conditional love or attention. For example, "I will stop arguing with you, if you give me what I want." When real experiences from the past are generalized to current events old coping strategies are the primary source of resolution.

Perceived expectations are grounded in familial, religious, cultural, and social norms. For example, a female may feel pressure to be sweet, quiet, assertive, passive, strong, modest, intelligent, supportive, hardworking, and maternal at the same time. These conflicting expectations create and promote a state of chaos, resulting in continual adaptation to meet the perceived beliefs of the moment.

Write about the various REAL roles/expectations you play in your life.

_____

_____

_____

_____

_____

═══

Write about the various PERCIEVED roles/expectations you play in your life.

_____

_____

_____

_____

_____

_____

═══

Who or what led you to believe that you must meet these expectations in order to be considered a good human?

_____

_____

_____

_____

_____

_____

6. IS IT SCIENCE?

The toxic box is comparable to a Skinner Box[5]. The Skinner Box was used in a psychological experiments that focused on learning. One of the experiments involved putting a hungry rat in a box where it was required to press a lever for a food pellet. This began as a simple task but as the rat travelled through several trails the complexity of the task increased.

This experiment demonstrated that when an animal is hungry they will take whatever steps necessary to be fed. The food pellets lead to the fulfillment of a physical need which creates a connection between the behavior and the desired outcome. In generalizing this concept to human behavior the *pellets* are emotional rather than physical. These emotional pellets represent anything that leads to a sense of validation and approval. Similar to the increasing complexity of tasks required by the rats in the Skinner Box trails, when a person is emotionally starved they will go to great lengths to be fed.

[5] Skinner, B. F. 1935. Two Types of Conditioned Reflex and a Pseudo Type. *Journal of General Psychology* 12: 66-77.

What *pellets* do you seek from others?

Check any that apply and add any *pellets* you seek from others that are not listed..

- Approval
- Attention
- Permission
- Security
- Identity
- Money
- Validation
- Affection
- Gifts
- Self-worth
- _____
- _____
- _____
- _____
- _____
- _____
- _____
- _____
- _____
- _____
- _____

Describe the patterns that have evolved from your efforts to obtain emotional pellets from another person .

For Example:

When I first met _____ *(name of person)* _____ everything was amazing! I was always encouraged and felt supported. We had so much in common and I thought I had met my soul mate. Overtime, the compliments faded and I felt I had to do more and more to get _____ *(name of person)* _____ 's attention. Now, I feel invisible. I am doing everything I can to repair the relationship but nothing seems to work. I feel so empty, alone, and exhausted.

_____

_____

_____

_____

_____

_____

_____

Describe your feelings associated with relationship dynamic.

_____

_____

_____

_____

_____

_____

_____

As previously mentioned, neither the giver nor the taker truly understands the concept of self-care, often resulting in the misconception that survival is obtained through dependency. The dynamic of a 90/10 relationship is reinforced by creating excitement, that leads to a senses of validation. Let's explore possible explanations for the continuation of toxic patterns.

Reinforcement #1

This is EXCITING stuff! The transition periods between the **Toxic Box** and **Isolation** are stimulating and often produce a large amount of emotional pellets in the form of power shifts, control, increased attention, and affection. Initially, this feels great but once the dust settles, old patterns reemerge and the relationship returns to status quo. The excitement is extreme and can often feel invigorating, even addicting. Viewing emotions on a scale of 1(awful) to 10 (amazing) creates an unhealthy, polarized dynamic with minimal in-between, where life is AWFUL (1) or AMAZING (10).

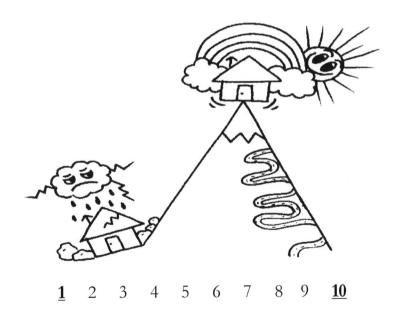

1 2 3 4 5 6 7 8 9 **10**

Many people justify unacceptable behaviors and situations because the **10** feels so amazing. This can be explained by understanding the basic learning principle of classical conditioning, involving a learned association between two events after they are repeatedly paired over a period of time. This results in a reflexive response to a given event.

The most basic example is the experiment conducted by Ivan Pavlov that focused on classical conditioning[6].

Step 1: **Food *causes* Salivation**

- Pavlov presented dogs with food and noted the dogs' response of salivation.

Step 2: **Food + Bell *causes* Salivation**

- Pavlov repeatedly paired a bell with the food, to which, the dog responded by salivating.

Step 3: **Bell *causes* Salivation**

- Pavlov would ring the bell without presenting food and the dogs would salivate. The dogs learned to expect food when they heard the bell, which triggered the reflexive response to salivate.

---

[6] Pavlov, P. I. (2010). Conditioned Reflexes: An Investigation of the Physiological Activity of the Cerebral Cortex. *Annals of Neurosciences, 17*(3), 136.

This concept can be applied to the 90/10 relationship. Positive moments are so often followed by negative moments that good times can trigger an anxious response. If an individual is conditioned to expect positive moments to end in a negative way they become anxious about positive experiences, in spite of the desire to have them. The anticipation anxiety associated with waiting for the positive moments to end can lead to self-sabotage, paranoia, shame, doubt, guilt, pessimism, anxiety, anger and self-fulfilling prophecies.

Example:

Step 1: **Negative Event (Silent Treatment)** *causes* **Anxiety**

- When you set a boundary with a colleague about not being able to stay late on Friday to help with a project, she gives you the silent treatment which causes feelings of anxiety.

Step 2: **Negative Event (Silent Treatment) + Positive Event (Attention)** *causes* **Fear**

- The following week your colleague appears to be in a great mood and asks you to join her for lunch. You are enjoying your time when she unexpectedly and without reason resumes the silent treatment. When you ask is some is wrong she replies by saying, "No, everything is fine." This results in feeling anxious and confused.

Step 3: **Positive Event (Attention)** *causes* **Fear**

- Later that afternoon your colleague offers you a cupcake that she picked up while on break. You feel anxious about the offer and she confronts you on your reactions. You feel confused because she has not done anything to warrant your feelings of anxiety. However, the previous experiences have solidified an expectation that a negative outcome is pending.

Reinforcement #2

Chaos and fear is familiar and offers a sense of certainty and stability. Many individuals seek out chaotic life patterns that are similar to those initiated at a young age and solidified throughout experiences and relationships. It is not uncommon for individuals to desire peace but then struggle to change unhealthy behavioral patterns that breed chaos and fear in their lives. Individuals who have learned to associate joy with pain find their quest for peace to especially difficult.

Step 1: **Traumatic experience** *causes* **Fear and anxiety for future trauma**

Step 2: **Experiencing a joyful moment and a traumatic experience happens** *causes* **Fear and anxiety for future trauma**

Step 3: **Peaceful moments** *cause* **Fear and anxiety for a future trauma**

Many individuals who have survived chaotic experiences are drawn to and often thrive in high stress careers such as emergency services, military, and upper management. These careers are highly stimulating and the ability to control the chaos creates a sense of stability and empowerment.

Does choosing a chaotic career promote a sense of control over chaos reinforce the need to stay in a dysfunctional system or is it a healthy outlet for chaotic energy?

_____

_____

_____

_____

_____

It is fully possible to have a stimulating career and life with plenty of controlled chaos and at the same time feel content and fulfilled. Chaotic energy can easily be used as a resource for enjoyable activities not just tragedy. However, it is about balance and one must understand that it will be difficult to find peace if they only practice chaos.

Changing lifelong patterns is similar to learning a foreign language. For example, English may be one's first language but that person may also like to speak Spanish. In order to speak another language fluently it is necessary to research, practice, and speak with others who know the language. Furthermore, it is important to expect and prepare for set-backs. Even with intense practice, it is likely that the new Spanish speaker will retreat to speaking English in moments of discomfort or pressure.

Living a peaceful life may feel intimidating because it is unfamiliar territory. The concepts of peace and stability are often associated with pain from repeated past experiences where good things *always* turned bad. Many admit to feeling safer when they are in danger. This grows from a history of persistent instability and the need to proactively prepare for the next *worst case scenario*. In a sense, individuals with this background actively keep themselves *primed for pain* in order to overcome the next tragic obstacle. This priming is evident in career choices, addictions, chaotic relationships, self-sabotage, anxiety, and extreme reactions to minor events. Being primed for pain prepares one for the worst-case scenario in order to maintain a sense of control and to minimize the chance of being caught off guard. Seeking and maintaining chaos is a defense strategy that prevents us from being surprised by unknown fiascos.

Perhaps, you know someone who panics over the smallest issues and appears to live on the verge of a mental break down. However, when an event occurs that would be deemed an emergency it is that person who is the most collected and able to flawlessly facilitate the situation. These individuals are likely to be primed for chaos by practicing with small events, allowing them to manage emergent situations with ease. Staying calm and level-headed during times of pandemonium is an extraordinary skill set but needs to be utilized only during emergencies. Managing (not eliminating) this coping strategy will provide you with confidence to explore other parts of yourself that are not so extreme.

If an emergency were to occur, have faith that your internal emergency management system (EMS) will be able to handle the situation, just as it has for the past ＿＿ years. Remember if chaos, similar to English, is your first language it does not need to be practiced. Now is a good time to thank your personal EMS and allow it to rest while you welcome other parts of yourself that are waiting to learn new ways to experience life.

Reinforcement #3

What keeps you in chaos?

_____

_____

_____

_____

_____

_____

How do you respond to peace?

_____

_____

_____

_____

_____

_____

_____

The lion believes that everyone shares his state of mind.

~ Mexican Proverb

Describe the role of your internal EMS.

_____
_____
_____
_____
_____
_____
_____
_____

Do you REALLY want peace?   CIRCLE one: YES   or   NO

If YES, what do you plan to do with it? If NO is it due to fear or bordom? Is is a little of both?

_____
_____
_____
_____
_____
_____
_____
_____

7. ISOLATION

It is not uncommon to want shut down when we find ourselves doing more and more to be emotionally fed without the desired results. When the pellets are no longer worth the effort, a transition occurs. Specifically, once the demands exceed the available resources, the giver transitions from the toxic box to a form of isolation. This change varies from person to person but regardless of the strategy, one becomes hopeful that leaving the toxic box will provide some relief.

What isolation tactics do you use to leave the Toxic Box?

Check all that apply to you. Jot down any tactics you use that are not listed below.

o Silent treatment	o "Shutting Down"
o Withdrawing	o Running Away
o Caretaking	o Passive Aggression
o Working	o _____
o Busy-ness	o _____
o Illness	o _____
o Migraines	o _____
o Self-harm	o _____
o Panic attacks	o _____
o Rage	o _____
o Depression	o _____

Transitioning from the toxic box to isolation provides temporary relief but is not sustainable. Shortly after entering isolation, the hunger for emotional fulfillment reemerges initiating an exploration of the costs vs. benefits of returning the toxic box. Returning may not be desirable but it is familiar and navigable.

The Conflict...

Isolation:

"I have a little control and some dignity but I am really hungry for attention."

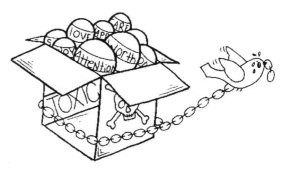

Toxic Box:

"This is exhausting but at least I am getting a little emotional food"

This dilemma creates a interesting challenge for the taker. Due to the taker's struggles with self-care, the exit of the giver elicits panic and fear. The experience of not being cared for is unsettling and often results in a temporary power shift. This shift is in response to the taker's dependency on the giver, making the giver's return to the toxic box a priority. Due to the takers discomfort and growing fear, various strategies are initiated to achieve this goal.

 The first approach is typically sweet and heartfelt, especially in the early stages of the *90/10* relationship. He or she offers an overload of emotional pellets in the form of love, apologies, presents, tears, affection, and/or promises. This gesture may be appealing but the ultimate goal is to move the giver back into the role of service.

Translation:

"I will give you a bunch of emotional pellets until you get back in the toxic box so we can settle back into our normal routine. I will drag this out as long as necessary, maybe two weeks, until things settled down. At that point you will return to giving 90% and I will return to giving 10%. Life will be good!"

If the giver denies the taker's efforts of kindness, a bullying tactic is often deployed. Both of these approaches are indicative of the taker's ultimate fear and inability of being responsible for themselves. The bullying tactics may include threatening, silent treatment, aggression, manipulation, and/or threats of replacement.

Translation:

"You will get back in the toxic box or you can stay where you are and starve. I can easily replace you because I have a lot to offer. In fact, I am doing you a favor by giving you the opportunity to be in the toxic box because no one else is going to want you."

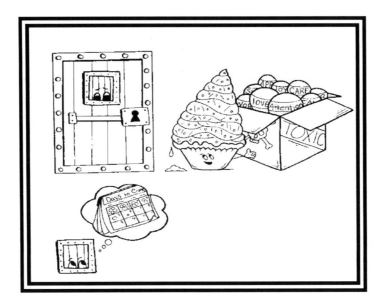

This decoding sounds dramatic but occurs frequently. How many times have you or someone you've known returned to toxic relationships after declaring *never again?*

The revolving door between isolation and the toxic box is draining and completely unhealthy.

You may go where you want,

but you cannot escape yourself.

~ Norwegian Proverb

If you want to know your future,

look at what you are doing in this moment.

~ Tibetan Proverb

8. CHOOSE YOUR HEALTHY NORMAL

Fortunately, there is a consistent and stable option for meeting needs of the givers and the takers. It is not as exciting as the extremes often experienced in an unhealthy relationship but it works; allowing you to establish a foundation from which you can effectively manage your life. This process involves making a decision about what *you* need and do not need in your life by determining what does and does not serve you. It may be an old habit to seek advice from others when defining your healthy normal but this is *not* the point. This is about your needs and what works for you. Suggestions will be offered but the goal is to reflect inwardly rather than relying on others to determine this for you.

Let's explore characteristics of a *healthy normal* relationship pattern. Relationships that are 50/50, meaning both parties contribute equal amounts of energy, are healthy relationships. Obviously, there is not a scale to measure if a relationship is in balance but the overall dynamic is balanced and both parties provide an equal contribution of effort. The natural ebb and flow of relationships requires flexibility and at times one person will provide more support the other. We all have 50/50 relationships in our life but they tend to be in the background because they require less energy than the 90/10 relationship. Healthy relationships are supportive, encouraging, present, and honest. In comparison to a toxic relationship which can feel like a hostage situation.

A Rule of Thumb:

✓ After an encounter with someone who is healthy you feel energized and confident. There is no question about the the status of the relationship.

✓ After an encounter with someone who is toxic you find yourself analyzing the details of the event to calculate the status of the relationship. Lingering thoughts about the encounter and a general sense of uneasiness is commonly experienced.

Create a list of healthy relationships in Column A and unhealthy relationships in Column B

Column A: Healthy Relationships	Column B: Unhealthy Relationships

The most important part of emotional health is taking ownership of self-care and maintaining a strong emotional immune system. Imagine the pictures with the jars below as a metaphor to illustrate this concept…

The jar represents your body and the beads represent your emotional immune system. When you are functioning from a healthy perspective you understand that it is *your* responsibility to keep yourself at least ½ full. Emotionally feeding yourself significantly decreases the need for chronic dependency on others. When a healthy person starts to feel low on inventory (beads) there is a plan of action to address the shortage. Self-care decreases dependency and it offers confidence to pursue personal interests that promote positive growth and happiness.

When you are unhealthy, and your jar is empty, feelings of emptiness lead to desperate attempts to receive emotional nourishment. This jar of beads may contain one or two beads that you received as a pellet from another person. This is not enough for emotional nourishment resulting in drastic measures and codependent behaviors.

New Pattern

Earlier, we looked at the 1-10 pattern to describe the extreme nature of an unhealthy normal. Now we will look at the 5-6 pattern as a means to describe the steady nature of a healthy normal pattern. Learning to live in the 5-6 zone is consistent, proactive, and self-directed. The 5-6 zone is not as extreme as the 1-10 pattern but it is manageable as it elicits a sense of certainty and security. The beauty is in the foundation you create for yourself. This foundation offers a sense of security and stability when life offers extremes.

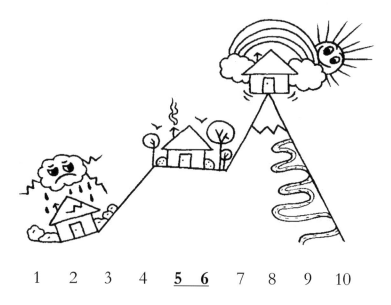

1   2   3   4   **5   6**   7   8   9   10

Some worry that living a lifestyle in the <u>5-6</u> zone will be boring, but when a person is is healthy they are able to experiencing exciting moments more frequently. The aftermath is simply returning to the <u>5-6</u> foundation. This is juxtaposed to the old view where an amazing (10) moment resulted in a plummet to the land of misery (1). When you experience a painful situation, you have the space to process and return to your foundation rather. Creating and taking command your <u>5-6</u> space allows you to fully experience your life.

What does a 5-6 lifestyle look like to you?

_____

_____

_____

_____

_____

_____

_____

What are your feelings and assumptions about a 5-6 lifestyle?

_____

_____

_____

_____

_____

_____

Change the way you look at things,

and the things you look at will change.

~ Buddhist Proverb

9. FINDING YOUR PATTERN

It may be difficult to see, but you already have several systems in place that serve you well. You are not starting from scratch! Your first job is to identify healthy behaviors and make them a priority. Metaphorically speaking, identify behaviors that allow you to add beads to your jar. What are your beads? Explore activities that promote a sense of wellness and will provide space and energy to enjoy and explore your wonderful world.

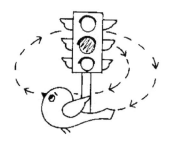

Many people spend their lives in a holding pattern waiting for the next task, chore, or performance. This holding pattern is pointless and will never result in feelings of fulfillment. Seriously, what are you waiting for? Life should not be a holding pattern, rather it should be experienced actively.

When you are emotionally well, small obstacles do not impact on your sense of well-being. If your physical immune system is weak then you are more susceptible to serious illness as opposed to when your immune system is strong. Likewise, we need strong emotional immune systems to function at our highest level. Each person is responsible for creating and implementing a healthy normal pattern for stability. It has nothing to do with what other people think you should or should not be. If we depend on others to guide us through this process, we will always feel uncertain and seek others' approval. There are always extremes when trying to please others.

For instance, imagine, one morning a woman prepares breakfast for her partner that includes two scrambled eggs and he responds by saying, "Thanks Sweetie, but I wanted poached eggs." The next morning, she adjusts by preparing two poached eggs and he responds by saying, "Oh thank you, but I wanted scrambled eggs." On the third morning she prepares one poached egg and one scrambled egg and her partner responds by saying, "Thanks, but you poached the wrong egg."

This is an example of how attempting to please others can be taken to the extreme. Unfortunately, it is common to encounter contradictory expectations on the journey to self-awareness leading to an intensified sense of insecurity and confusion.

For example:

If you...	Others may say or imply...
Are thin	You need to gain weight
Are overweight	You need to lose weight
Talk fast	Slow Down
Talk Slowly	Speed up
Work hard	You're a workaholic
Don't make work a priority	You are lazy

What are some of the contradictions that you experience?

When I...	Others say or imply...

These contradictions further increase the importance of determining what works for you. When you find what works, do more of it! When what you are doing stops working, change it.

Write about your thoughts on the contradictory messages received by others.

_____

_____

_____

_____

_____

_____

_____

_____

Identifying a healthy normal is similar to knowing your vital signs. Begin by identifying simple activities that can be completed on a regular basis. Below are some examples. Pick the any that have made you feel positive about yourself. This list is by no means exclusive so be sure to add your vitals to the list.

- Specific bed time
- Specific wake up time
- Shower in the AM or PM
- Alcohol vs. No Alcohol
- Diet
- Exercise
- Reading
- Spending time with family
- Church attendance
- Attend meetings
- Therapy appointments
- Cooking
- Spending time with pets
- Work

- Time in nature
- Meditation
- Daily reflection
- Reading with my kids
- _____
- _____
- _____
- _____
- _____
- _____
- _____
- _____

The simplicity of this model can be a little unnerving but the goal is to take care of your basic needs in attempt to prevent preoccupation with negativity. It is easy to lose sight of everything in our healthy normal when we are being co-dependent. Below is an example of one individual's healthy normal laid out in a schedule.

	MON	TUES	WED	THUR	FRI	SAT	SUN
Wake up at 6:15am							
Make my Bed							
"Me" Time (6:15am – 7:00am)							
Morning Reflection							
Prepare and Eat Breakfast with Kids							
Leave Work at 3:00pm							
Emails (3:30pm-4:00pm)							
Keep the House Neat							
Exercise Daily							
Mindful Eating							
Sobriety							
Prepare for Tomorrow							
Shower at Night							
Sleep at 10:00pm							

KEEP IT SIMPLE!

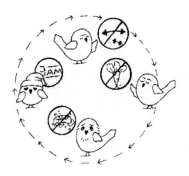

The objective is to engage in behaviors that serve your well-being and make them a priority. Understand that one missed activity does not equate to a crisis but be aware of the impact that discounting self-care has on your overall sense of well-being.

Example: "Because <u>(ENTER EXCUSE HERE)</u>, I am not going to exercise today which could lead to not eating well, not showering at night, not sleeping well, and sleeping late."

List some of your most commonly used excuses to avoid self-care.

_____

_____

_____

_____

_____

_____

_____

_____

_____

_____

What are your indicators that you arte lacking in self-care?

_____

_____

_____

_____

_____

_____

_____

How will you use this information to make changes?

_____

_____

_____

_____

_____

_____

_____

10. U-TURNS AND WARNING FLAGS

Re-entering toxic patterns does *not* warrant a crisis as long as there is awareness and an understanding of how to recover. Without awareness and a plan, a lack of self-care can quickly lead to a downward spiral resulting in self-defeating habits.

One strategy for increasing awareness is to identify warning flags. Warning flags signal a deviation from healthy living and are often a direct route to the toxic box. These warning signals are often uncomfortable but they can be helpful.

Warning flags signal that a U-turn is immanent. If we are going to stay on track, we have to keep ourselves healthy. Who has the time or energy to waste in the toxic box? When we are in the toxic box we miss out on our lives as preoccupation with chaos impairs the ability to fully experience the treasures in our lives including children, friends, family, pets, hobbies, travel, spirituality, creativity, etc. There is no reason to continue wasting time with situations that will never warrant positive outcomes. The effort that is needed to navigate and manage a toxic lifestyle would have surely resulted in a positive outcome by now, if it was possible. It is time to focus all that energy on the relationships and activities that are fulfilling and promote joy.

What are some of your warning signs?

Check all that apply and add other signs not listed.

o   Seeking Approval

o   Comparison

o   Jealousy

o   Asking Permission

o   Justifying

o   Making Excuses

o   Saying "Screw it!"

o   _____

o   _____

o   _____

o   _____

o   _____

o   _____

o   _____

o   _____

With practice, making U-turns and getting back to business will become second nature. Others may make assume your efforts towards self-care are offensive and selfish which may lead to actions of discouragement. Self-care is not a personal attack towards others, it is simply our personal responsibility to be healthy. If another person takes issue with your commitment for self-care, then it is clear they should be doing their own self-exploration.

back to my business

Example:

Imagine a person with a peanut allergy is offered a peanut butter cookie, they say "no," choosing not to eat the peanut butter cookie. This is a self-care issue and not a personal attack against the person who offered the cookie. If the person offering the cookie is offended, then clearly they have a serious issue that you most likely are not professionally trained to address.

When another person is offended by your self-care, you have a clear indication that you are dealing with a 90/10 relationship. You'll notice that your 50/50 relationships will be supportive in this situation. Toxic people need your energy, even when you don't have any to give. These individuals may resort to old tricks to get you to return to the toxic box. Acknowledging these behaviors will contribute to positive boundaries, showing a commitment to your self-care, and freedom to disengage from unhealthy behaviors. Be mindful that in the beginning, self-care may resemble previous retreats to isolation but it is quite the opposite. When a person is healthy they emotionally sustain themselves, dissolving the need to obtain emotional pellets from others.

When you are healthy, the toxic people in your life consequently leave or adapt in response to your boundaries. That's okay. Actually, it is great! Eventually, takers will realize they can't get their needs met from you and will seek it elsewhere or explore their own self-care options. Their leaving is not an insult, but a part of the process. How the takers choses to handle your boundaries is not your concern. If they get angry and have a tantrum, let them. Give yourself permission to disengage and allow them to behave in whatever way they choose, just not in your space. You have plenty of things to do while they throw a fit if that is how they choose to respond. If they insist on throwing a fit in your space, then remove yourself in order to prevent unnecessary distress.

If you define yourself as a taker and are seeking change to to increasingly maladaptive behaviors, be aware that you have a unique challenges. Setting limits with a a giver can be complicated due to expectations they require from their caretaking efforts. If you are overwhelmed and need a break or space, then take it!

Everyone needs to find balance. How the givers in your life choose to handle your boundaries is no longer your concern. You will have to limit the habit of accepting everything you are given. Simply and kindly communicate your intentions and allow yourself to say "no, thank-you." The primary goal of practicing self-care is to discontinue dependency on others and to build confidence in your ability to generate a sense of personal well-being.

Write about a situation or situations that it would be in your best interest to tell someone "no."

_____

_____

_____

_____

_____

_____

_____

_____

_____

_____

_____

The borrower is servant to the lender.

~ Biblical Proverb

What are your concerns about saying "no"?

_____
_____
_____
_____
_____
_____
_____
_____
_____
_____
_____

List your strategies for overcoming those concerns?

_____

_____

_____

_____

_____

_____

_____

_____

_____

_____

_____

_____

_____

_____

_____

THOUGHT SPOT

11. TWO-WEEK CHALLENGE

The two-week challenge is designed to jump start your practice of a healthier you. You have discovered a pattern of behaviors that work and don't work. Now it is time put this knowledge into practice.

Before starting this challenge, complete the Satisfaction with Life Scale[7] (located on pg. 86) to determine a baseline of your current level of happiness. After completing the Satisfaction with Life Scale create a list of healthy behaviors that serve your higher purpose. Throughout the two weeks, you will track the frequency in which you engaged in the activities that you determined to be an important part of your self-care. Along with tracking your daily activities you should spend a few minutes each day reflecting on your goals, grievances, and gratitudes from the day. This reflection provides an opportunity to explore progress as well as areas that need attention. Once you complete the challenge, retake the assessment (located on pg. 93) to assess if you experienced a positive change in your quality of life.

Remember the purpose of this activity is to start your practice of self-care. Practice is an ongoing process that is focused on a specific intention. Your intention is personal and there are no specific guidelines for setting your intention except staying focused on the goal of living a more peaceful existence.

---

[7] Diener, E., Emmons, R. A., Larsen, R. J., & Griffin, S. (1985). The Satisfaction with Life Scale. *Journal of Personality Assessment, 49*, 71-7

List your intention(s) for this practice.

_____

_____

_____

_____

_____

_____

_____

_____

List some possible outcomes you are looking forward to and are seeking as a result of the two-week challenge.

_____

_____

_____

_____

_____

_____

_____

_____

_____

It is common to have concerns when starting something new. Transition is difficult, even an exciting one. Be honest with yourself about your concerns of practicing a healthier version of yourself.

List your concerns about starting your practice.

_____

_____

_____

_____

_____

_____

_____

_____

_____

_____

_____

_____

They tried to bury us. They didn't know we were seeds.

~ Mexican proverb

Create a cost vs. benefit list to help you stay on track throughout the process of the two-week challenge.

BENEFITS of practicing my pattern for peace.

COSTS of ignoring my pattern for peace

13. TWO-WEEK CHALLENGE EXAMPLE

Week 1

Date: _____

I take care of myself by…

	MON	TUE	WED	THUR	FRI	SAT	SUN
Maintaining my Yard							
Morning Meditation							
Arrive to work 10 Minutes Early							
Yoga at least 3/week							
No Dirty Dishes in the Sink							
Cleaning my House – 20 minutes per day							
Daily Hygiene							
Reading with my Kids							
Being in Nature							
Daily Reflection							
No Alcohol at Home							
Having Coffee with my Husband							
Connecting with Others							
Changing my Sheets Weekly							

	GOALS	✔
MON	Attend a yoga class.	
TUES	Arrive to work 20 minutes early.	
WED	Limit screen time to 30 minutes.	
THUR	Catch up with friends.	
FRI	Finish all my paperwork before leaving the office.	
SAT	Take a hike with my family.	
SUN	Prepare my children's outfits for the week.	

	GRIEVENCES
MON	I was late to work.
TUES	Traffic!
WED	Careless mistakes with paperwork.
THUR	Struggled with time management.
FRI	I had to work later than I expected.
SAT	It rained all day.
SUN	I need more help with housework.

	GRATITUDES
MON	The day went smoothly.
TUES	I learned several new ideas during a training today and I can use them with my clients.
WED	I had 3 awesome sessions with my clients.
THURS	I completed a huge project and felt a sense of relief.
FRI	I had a great time with my friends and did not stay up too late.
SAT	My family and I went to a play and had a great time.
SUN	I am grateful for my family and the time I spent with them today.

14. PRACTICING MY PATTERN

Satisfaction with Life Scale[8]

Below are five statements that you may agree or disagree with. Using the 1 - 7 scale below, indicate your agreement with each item by placing the appropriate number on the line preceding that item. Please be open and honest in your responding.

- 7 - Strongly agree
- 6 - Agree
- 5 - Slightly agree
- 4 - Neither agree nor disagree
- 3 - Slightly disagree
- 2 - Disagree
- 1 - Strongly disagree

_____ In most ways my life is close to my ideal.

_____ The conditions of my life are excellent.

_____ I am satisfied with my life.

_____ So far I have gotten the important things I want in life.

_____ If I could live my life over, I would change almost nothing.

Add your answers to get your total score.

- 31 - 35 Extremely satisfied
- 26 - 30 Satisfied
- 21 - 25 Slightly satisfied
- 20   Neutral
- 15 - 19 Slightly dissatisfied
- 10 - 14 Dissatisfied
- 5 - 9   Extremely dissatisfied

*See Appendix A for a full description of the scores for The Satisfaction with Life Scale.

---

[8] Diener, E., Emmons, R. A., Larsen, R. J., & Griffin, S. (1985). The Satisfaction with Life Scale. *Journal of Personality Assessment, 49,* 71-7

Week 1

Date: _____

I take care of myself by...

	MON	TUE	WED	THUR	FRI	SAT	SUN

	GOALS	✔
MON		
TUES		
WED		
THUR		
FRI		
SAT		
SUN		

	GRIEVENCES
MON	
TUES	
WED	
THUR	
FRI	
SAT	
SUN	

	GRATITUDES
MON	
TUES	
WED	
THURS	
FRI	
SAT	
SUN	

Week 2

Date: _____

I take care of myself by…

	MON	TUE	WED	THUR	FRI	SAT	SUN

	GOALS	✔
MON		
TUES		
WED		
THUR		
FRI		
SAT		
SUN		

	GRIEVENCES
MON	
TUES	
WED	
THUR	
FRI	
SAT	
SUN	

	GRATITUDES
MON	
TUES	
WED	
THURS	
FRI	
SAT	
SUN	

Satisfaction with Life Scale[9]

Below are five statements that you may agree or disagree with. Using the 1 - 7 scale below, indicate your agreement with each item by placing the appropriate number on the line preceding that item. Please be open and honest in your responding.

- 7 - Strongly agree
- 6 - Agree
- 5 - Slightly agree
- 4 - Neither agree nor disagree
- 3 - Slightly disagree
- 2 - Disagree
- 1 - Strongly disagree

_____ In most ways my life is close to my ideal.

_____ The conditions of my life are excellent.

_____ I am satisfied with my life.

_____ So far I have gotten the important things I want in life.

_____ If I could live my life over, I would change almost nothing.

Add your answers to get your total score.

- 31 - 35 Extremely satisfied
- 26 - 30 Satisfied
- 21 - 25 Slightly satisfied
- 20   Neutral
- 15 - 19 Slightly dissatisfied
- 10 - 14 Dissatisfied
- 5 - 9   Extremely dissatisfied

*See Appendix 1 for a full description of the scores for The Satisfaction with Life Scale

---

[9] Diener, E., Emmons, R. A., Larsen, R. J., & Griffin, S. (1985). The Satisfaction with Life Scale. *Journal of Personality Assessment, 49,* 71-7

15. CONTINUED PRACTICE

Congratulations on starting your practice towards your new version of normal. Hopefully, at this point, your intentions are solidified and you are gaining an awareness about the necessity of self-care. On the next few pages you can explore and process your journey.

You have experienced some changes in your social dynamics. Some people may have been supportive while others were resistant to your work. Take a moment and write about the reactions from others in response to your changes.

_____

_____

_____

_____

_____

_____

_____

_____

_____

Fall seven times, stand up eight.

~ Japanese Proverb

What surprised you the most about this journey?

_____

_____

_____

_____

_____

_____

_____

_____

_____

_____

Describe the most difficult part of this experience?

_____

_____

_____

_____

_____

_____

_____

_____

_____

_____

Describe the most satisfying part of this experience?

_____

_____

_____

_____

_____

_____

Discuss the differences in your expectations vs. the reality of the two-week challenge.

_____

_____

_____

_____

_____

_____

To conclude your work, briefly summarize your understanding of choosing a Healthy Normal

_____

_____

_____

_____

_____

_____

Think of one word, design, or short phrase to summarize your practice and to assist you in continuing your work. This word or phrase can be used as a mantra: a simple reminder to keep you grounded throughout your practice. The mantra emphasizes your intention.. Your job is to practice being YOU!

My Mantra...

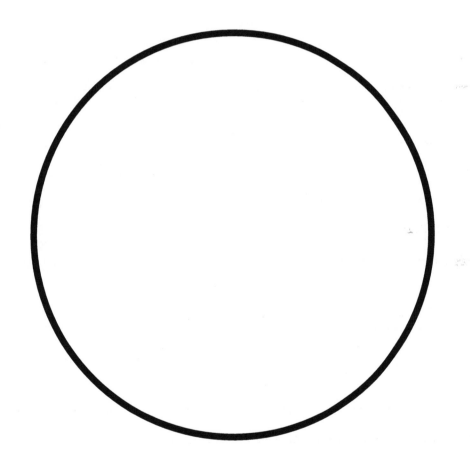

APPENDIX

Understanding Scores on Diener's Satisfaction with Life Scale by Ed Diner

30 – 35 Very high score; highly satisfied

Respondents who score in this range love their lives and feel that things are going very well. Their lives are not perfect, but they feel that things are about as good as lives get. Furthermore, just because the person is satisfied does not mean she or he is complacent. In fact, growth and challenge might be part of the reason the respondent is satisfied. For most people in this high-scoring range, life is enjoyable, and the major domains of life, work or school, family, friends, leisure, and personal development.

25- 29 High score

Individuals who score in this range like their lives and feel that things are going well. Of course their lives are not perfect, but they feel that things are mostly good. Furthermore, just because the person is satisfied does not mean she or he is complacent. In fact, growth and challenge might be part of the reason the respondent is satisfied. For most people in this high-scoring range, life is enjoyable, and the major domains of life, work or school, family, friends, leisure, and personal development. The person may draw motivation from the areas of dissatisfaction.

20 – 24 Average score

The average of life satisfaction in economically developed nations are in this range. The majority of people are generally satisfied, but have some areas where they very much would like some improvement. Individuals that score in this range are either mostly satisfied with most areas of their lives but see the need for some improvement in each area; or they are satisfied with most domains of their lives, but have one or two areas where they would like to see large improvements. A person scoring in this range is normal in that they have areas of their lives that need improvement. Most individuals in this range would usually like to move to a higher level by making some life changes.

15 – 19 Slightly below average life satisfaction

People who score in this range have small but significant problems in several areas of their lives, or have many areas that are doing fine but one area that represents a substantial problem for them. If a person has moved temporarily into this level of life satisfaction from a higher level because of some recent event, things will usually improve over time and satisfaction will generally move back up. On the other hand, if a person is chronically slightly dissatisfied with many areas of life, some changes might be in order. Sometimes the person is expecting too much, and life changes are needed. Although temporary dissatisfaction is common and normal, a chronic level of dissatisfaction across a number of areas of life calls for reflection. Some people can gain motivation from a small level of dissatisfaction, but often dissatisfaction across a number of life domains is a distraction.

10 – 14 Dissatisfied

People who score in this range are substantially dissatisfied with their lives. People in this range may have a number of domains that are not going well, or one or two domains that are going very badly. If life dissatisfaction is a response to a recent event such as bereavement, divorce, or a significant problem at work, the person will probably return over time to his or her former level of higher satisfaction. If low levels of life satisfaction have been chronic for the person, some changes should be made in attitudes, patterns of thinking, and in life activities. Persisting low levels of life satisfaction in this range can indicate that things are going badly and life alterations are needed. A person with low life satisfaction is sometimes not functioning well because their unhappiness serves as a distraction. Talking to a friend, member of the clergy, counselor, or other specialist can often help the person move in the right direction. Positive changes will be up to the person to implement and maintain.

5 – 9 Extremely Dissatisfied

Individuals who score in this range are extremely unhappy with their current life. In some cases, this is in reaction to some recent bad event such as widowhood, recently having lost a loved one, or unemployment. In other cases, it is a response to a chronic problem such as alcoholism or addiction. Dissatisfaction at this level is often due to dissatisfaction in multiple areas of life. It may be that the help of others is needed – a friend or family member, counseling with a member of the clergy, or help from a psychologist or other counselor. If the dissatisfaction is chronic, the person needs to change, and often others can help.

Part that is common to each category:

To understand life satisfaction scores, it is helpful to understand some of the components that go into most people's experience of satisfaction. One of the most important influences on happiness is social relationships. People who score high on the life satisfaction scale tend to have close and supportive loved ones, whereas those who do not have close loved ones are more likely to be dissatisfied. Of course the loss of a close friend or family member can cause dissatisfaction with life, and it may take time for the person to bounce back from the loss.

Other factors that influence the life satisfaction of most people are work, school, or performance in an important role such as homemaker or grandparent. When the person enjoys his or her work, whether it is paid or unpaid work, and feels that it is meaningful and important, this contributes to life satisfaction. When work is going poorly because of bad circumstances or a poor fit with the person's strengths, this can lower life satisfaction. When a person has important goals, and is failing to make adequate progress toward them, this too can lead to life dissatisfaction.

Still more factors that influence the life satisfaction of most people are personal, such as satisfaction with the self, religious or spiritual life, learning, growth, and leisure. For many people these are sources of satisfaction. When these sources of personal worth are frustrated, they can be powerful sources of dissatisfaction. There are additional sources of satisfaction and dissatisfaction – some that are common to most people such as health, and others that are unique to each individual. Most people know the factors that lead to their satisfaction or dissatisfaction, although a person's temperament can color their responses.

There is no one key to life satisfaction, but rather a recipe that includes a number of ingredients. With time and persistent work, people's life satisfaction usually goes up when they are dissatisfied. People who have had a loss recover over time. People who have a dissatisfying relationship often make changes over time that will increase their happiness. One key ingredient is social relationships. Another key ingredient is having goals that derive from one's values, and making progress toward those goals. For many people it is important to feel connected to something larger than oneself. When a person tends to be chronically dissatisfied, they should look within themselves and ask whether they need to develop more positive attitudes to life and the world.

From the Author

My name is Sarah Wickman Freeman, MA, Licensed Professional Clinical Counselor (LPCC). Over the past 10 years, the most common sentiment I have heard from clients is "I just want to be normal." This usually comes from individuals who are exhausted and overwhelmed. I have heard the statement reverberating in my mind countless days and nights and those echoes of struggle encouraged me to create this book. It is designed as a response to the success reported by those who have actively used these techniques and my personal desire to assist others in search for a healthier, more fulfilling "normal."

Illustrated by Anna Rebecca Waychoff

I have struggled with my own issues and have empathy and understanding for those with similar problems. I have discovered my own patterns and wanted to help others find their way. Being able to illustrate these ideas and bring them to life with a simplistic humor is a joy to me. I hope that the practical solutions in this book help all who read it.

Revised by Heather Webb, CSW

As a clinician specializing in trauma with children and adults, I find the content of this book very useful in assisting my clients with regaining a sense of ownership of their emotions and their future. In a society that is about doing more and being more, even if that is contraindicative of our personal goals, having a guide to regaining connection with oneself is not only relevant but also necessary.

Edited by Megan Gammon Algie, B.A.

I hold a B.A. in English and History from Western Kentucky University. I am a devoted mother, yoga devotee, and a survivor of childhood trauma. I am glad to lend my talents to this book as the techniques discussed have been beneficial to my own journey.

Made in the USA
Columbia, SC
10 November 2021